Dover Public Library
Dover, Delaware 19901
302-736-7030

CONTINENTS

EUROPE

by Suzanne Francis

Content Consultant
Eric Dorn Brose, PhD
Professor of History
Drexel University

CORE
LIBRARY

Published by ABDO Publishing Company, PO Box 398166, Minneapolis, MN 55439. Copyright © 2014 by Abdo Consulting Group, Inc. International copyrights reserved in all countries. No part of this book may be reproduced in any form without written permission from the publisher. The Core Library™ is a trademark and logo of ABDO Publishing Company.

Printed in the United States of America,
North Mankato, Minnesota
052013
092013

THIS BOOK CONTAINS AT LEAST 10% RECYCLED MATERIALS.

Editor: Blythe Hurley
Series Designer: Becky Daum

Library of Congress Control Number: 2013931973

Cataloging-in-Publication Data
Francis, Suzanne.
 Europe / Suzanne Francis.
   p. cm. -- (Continents)
ISBN 978-1-61783-932-0 (lib. bdg.)
ISBN 978-1-61783-997-9 (pbk.)
1. Europe--Juvenile literature.   I. Title.
940--dc23
                                        2013931973

Photo Credits: Boris Stroujko/Shutterstock Images, cover, 1; Red Line Editorial, 4, 12, 22; Ioan Panaite/Shutterstock Images, 6; Shutterstock Images, 8, 11, 12, 23, 33, 36, 42 (bottom), 43 (top), 43 (middle), 45; Javier Soto Vazquez/Shutterstock Images, 14; Sergey Toronto/Shutterstock Images, 16; Martin Fischer/Shutterstock Images, 19; Jamen Percy/Shutterstock Images, 20; European Commission, 22; Andrew Astbury/Shutterstock Images, 24; Ivan Montero Martinez/Shutterstock Images, 28; Andrei Nekrassov/Shutterstock Images, 30; Leonid Andronov/Shutterstock Images, 39; Nataliya Hora/Shutterstock Images, 41; Marc Scott-Parkin/Shutterstock Images, 42 (top); Ann Johansson/Corbis/AP Images, 42 (middle); Sorin Colac/Shutterstock Images, 43 (bottom)

CONTENTS

QUICK FACTS ABOUT EUROPE

- **Highest point:** Elbrus, a dormant Russian volcano, 18,510 ft (5,642 m)

- **Area:** 3,837,083 sq mi (9,938,000 sq km)

- **Distance north to south:** 2,076 miles (3,341 km)

- **Distance east to west:** 1,339 miles (2,155 km)

- **Key industries:** metal, petroleum, coal

- **Population:** 503,824,373

- **Five biggest cities:** Moscow, Russia; London, United Kingdom; St. Petersburg, Russia; Berlin, Germany; Madrid, Spain

- **Four most common languages:** German, English, Russian, French

- **Number of countries:** 47

ONE BIG PENINSULA

The continent of Europe is almost completely surrounded by water. Between the Arctic and Atlantic Oceans and the Mediterranean, Black, and Caspian Seas, there is water on almost every side of Europe. The Ural Mountains separate Europe from Asia in the country of Russia.

Europe has many different landscapes and climates. It has beautiful islands such as Sicily,

The Arc de Triomphe, an 1836 monument in Paris, France, is surrounded by modern automobile traffic on the Champs-Élysées, one of the most famous streets in the world.

The area known as the Giant's Causeway in Northern Ireland is a popular tourist destination and has been named a UNESCO World Heritage Site.

Ireland, and Iceland. There are peninsulas such as the Scandinavian, Iberian, and Balkan. A peninsula is a piece of land surrounded by water on three sides. The whole continent of Europe is actually one big peninsula.

Europe is the second smallest continent in the world, after Australia. It is also home to both the world's largest and smallest countries. Russia, which is in both Europe and Asia, is the largest country in the world. Vatican City is the smallest country in the world. This entire country is inside the city of Rome, Italy.

Ancient Fingerprints

Europeans have had a huge impact on world history. Many ideas and discoveries that first came from Europe have spread throughout the world. Most people believe ancient Greek culture laid the foundation for Western civilization. Ancient Greek society reached its height between 500 and 300 BCE. Ancient Greeks are known for their theater, political thought, the Olympics, math, and the alphabet. The ancient Greeks and Romans were also known for their military conquests.

The Roman Empire reached its height from 30 BCE to 180 CE. The Romans were amazing builders and thinkers. They developed concrete and plumbing. They built roads, bridges, and buildings that still stand today.

Throughout history, Europeans have been known for their art, music, and literature. Artists such as Leonardo da Vinci and Michelangelo transformed the visual arts. Composers

An Ancient Mystery

The ancient structure known as Stonehenge near the town of Salisbury, England, is a mystery. Why were these giant stones arranged in a horseshoe shape inside a circle? Who built it, and how? No one knows. Historians believe Stonehenge took more than 30 million hours to build. Was the site an ancient calendar? Or perhaps a place of worship? Stonehenge has been around for close to 5,000 years. But modern humans have yet to unlock its secrets.

The mysterious monument of Stonehenge in Great Britain remains a mystery to historians.

Wolfgang Amadeus Mozart and Ludwig van Beethoven changed the world of music. Famous English playwright and poet William Shakespeare was one of the founders of modern theater.

Hot Spot

Europe's many landmarks attract visitors from across the globe. Ancient sites such as the Parthenon in Greece and England's mysterious Stonehenge fascinate people around the world. From the snowy

oculus

coffers

recesses for sculptures

support columns

The Pantheon

Ancient Romans built the Pantheon between 27 BCE and 128 CE. This highly detailed building features a large dome with a circular opening at the top called an oculus that lets in light. After reading about the Romans, what did you imagine their buildings would look like? Did looking at this photo change your ideas about Roman architecture?

mountains of the Swiss Alps to the beaches of the French and Italian Riviera, Europe is full of incredible places.

Norwegian mythology is an ancient part of European culture. This story from *D'Aulaires' Book of Norse Myths* by Ingri and Edgar Parin d'Aulaire tells the tale of the beginning of the world:

> *Early in the morning of time there was no sand, no grass, no lapping wave. There was no earth, no sun, no moon, no stars. There was Niflheim, a waste of frozen fog, and Muspelheim, a place of raging flames. And in between the fog and fire there was a gaping pit—Ginungagap.*
>
> *For untold ages crackling embers from Muspelheim and crystals of ice from Niflheim whirled around in the dark and dismal pit. As they whirled together, faster and faster, fire kindled a spark of life within the ice. An enormous, ugly shape rose roaring from Ginungagap. It was the frost giant, Ymir, first of the race of the jotuns.*

Source: Ingri and Edgar Parin d'Aulaire. D'Aulaires' Book of Norse Myths. New York: New York Review of Books, 1967. Print. 12–14.

Consider Your Audience

Read the passage above closely. How could you adapt this story's words for a modern audience, such as your classmates? Write a blog post telling this same story to your new audience. What is the most effective way to get your point across to this audience? How is the language you use for the new audience different from the original text? Why?

CHAPTER TWO

SO MUCH WATER

Since Europe is a big peninsula, many different bodies of water touch it. The Atlantic Ocean is to the west. The Arctic Ocean is to the north.

Boundaries in Europe are often formed by bodies of water. The Strait of Gibraltar separates Europe from Africa. The strait is a small section of water that connects the Atlantic Ocean and the Mediterranean

The sun sets over the coast of the Strait of Gibraltar, the narrow strip of water that connects the Mediterranean Sea to the Atlantic Ocean and separates Spain in Europe from Morocco in Africa.

The Ural Mountains are rich in various natural resources, including metal ores, coal, and precious and semiprecious stones.

Sea. The Mediterranean Sea also divides southern Europe from Africa.

The Black Sea is in the southeastern part of Europe. Countries including Turkey, Bulgaria, Romania, Ukraine, and Russia surround the Black Sea. The Norwegian Sea and the North Sea are in northern Europe. Countries including Iceland, Norway, and the United Kingdom are on the Norwegian and North Seas.

The Ural Mountains stand between Europe and Asia. Since these two continents are connected by land, many people call them Eurasia. The countries of Russia and Turkey are in both Europe and Asia.

Lakes, Rivers, and Seas

Lakes cover only 2 percent of Europe. Most of Europe's lakes are in Finland, Sweden, Norway, and Russia. In fact, some people call Finland the Land of a Thousand Lakes. The country has more than 150,000 lakes. Lake Ladoga in Russia is the largest lake in

Europe. It has a surface area of almost 6,834 square miles (17,700 sq km).

Europe's many rivers connect these lakes, seas, and oceans. The Danube River empties into the Black Sea. The Rhine flows to the North Sea. The Volga River is the longest river in Europe. It is almost 2,299 miles (3,700 km) long. The Volga River flows through Russia. It empties into the Caspian Sea.

The Caspian Sea is not really a sea. It is the largest lake in the world. It is so big the ancient Greeks thought it was an ocean. That is how it got its name.

The Heart of Russia

Russians are very proud of the Volga River. Eleven of Russia's twenty largest cities are situated near the Volga. This includes Moscow, Russia's capital. Artists have created songs, stories, and paintings about the Volga. Some people compare it to the Mississippi River in the United States.

Europe's Mountain Ranges

The Alps are a mountain range in central Europe.

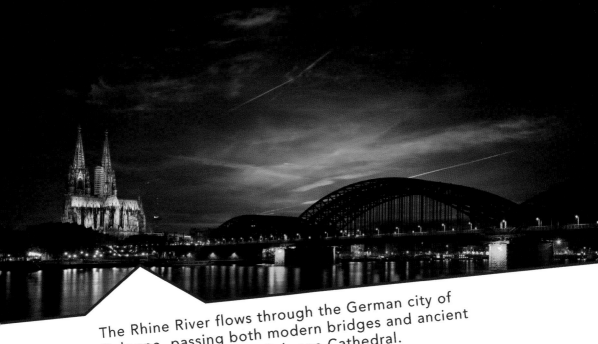

The Rhine River flows through the German city of Cologne, passing both modern bridges and ancient structures such as the Cologne Cathedral.

They are approximately 750 miles (1,200 km) long. The Alps are a part of ten countries. At 15,771 feet (4,807 m), Mont Blanc is the highest mountain in the Alps.

The Carpathian Mountains in central and eastern Europe are approximately 900 miles (1,450 km) long. The highest peaks in this range exceed 8,530 feet (2,600 m).

The Pyrenees Mountains form a natural border between the countries of France and Spain. The Pyrenees extend for approximately 270 miles

The northern lights, or aurora borealis, dance over a lake in Norway.

(435 km). At 11,168 feet (3,404 m), Pico de Aneto is the highest mountain in this range.

The Ural Mountains create a natural boundary between Europe and Asia. They run for approximately 1,553 miles (2,500 km) through western Russia.

Their highest point is Mount Narodnaya at 6,217 feet (1,895 m).

How's the Weather?

Most Europeans enjoy very mild weather. There are four different climates in Europe. These are the maritime, transitional, continental, and Mediterranean.

The maritime climate covers the area from Iceland to Ireland, western France, northern Germany, and northwestern Spain. These areas have a lot of rain throughout the year. Rainfall is especially heavy in autumn and winter. Summers are warm and can get fairly hot.

Central Europe has a transitional climate.

Natural Wonder

An aurora is a natural display of light in the sky. These displays happen most frequently in the polar regions. In the north this phenomenon is known as aurora borealis, or the northern lights. Auroras are caused by particles and radiation from the sun colliding with the earth's magnetic fields. Auroras can be seen by people in northern Europe.

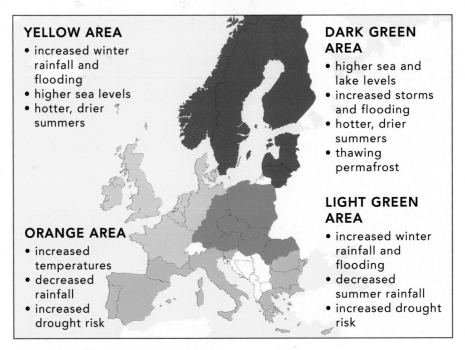

YELLOW AREA
- increased winter rainfall and flooding
- higher sea levels
- hotter, drier summers

DARK GREEN AREA
- higher sea and lake levels
- increased storms and flooding
- hotter, drier summers
- thawing permafrost

LIGHT GREEN AREA
- increased winter rainfall and flooding
- decreased summer rainfall
- increased drought risk

ORANGE AREA
- increased temperatures
- decreased rainfall
- increased drought risk

Climate Change in Europe

Much of Europe now enjoys mild weather suitable for farming. But scientists working for the European Union believe changing weather patterns will have serious negative consequences for European agriculture in the immediate future. How do you think the predicted changes shown on this map might affect farmers? How would those same problems affect the price of food in these areas?

This area includes central Sweden, southern Finland, eastern France, southwestern Germany, and most of central and southeastern Europe. The winters are cold, but things heat up in the summer. The weather varies depending on the altitude.

The mild Mediterranean climate makes southern Europe, including the Tuscany area in Italy, particularly good for farmland.

The continental climate covers much of Europe. Finland and northern Sweden, Russia, and northern Ukraine have a continental climate. People who live in these areas get roughly 10 to 20 inches (25 to 51 cm) of rain a year. Most of this rain falls in the summer. The winters here are longer and colder than anywhere else in Europe.

People in Italy and parts of France and Spain enjoy the Mediterranean climate. This climate has mild, wet winters. Summers are hot and dry.

ANIMALS AND PLANTS

Europe has varied climates and landscapes. It is no surprise a wide range of animals and plants live on the continent.

An Ice-Cold Desert

The European tundra covers approximately 88 percent of Iceland. It also runs along the Arctic coast in northern Russia and Scandinavia. The weather on the

A female white-tailed eagle snatches up a fish from a lake in Norway.

tundra is extreme. Winter lasts for ten months. During the summer the sun does not set for weeks.

Scientists consider the tundra to be a desert because it gets so little rain. But this desert is not hot. The ground in these areas stays frozen almost year-round. This frozen ground is called permafrost. Only certain types of plants can grow under these conditions. These include mosses, lichens, and ferns. Animals such as reindeer, arctic hares, and polar bears live in the tundra.

Forests

Long ago, forests covered most of Europe. As human populations grew, people cleared many

Reindeer Walkers

The Sami are an indigenous people from northern Europe. They have called this frosty region home for thousands of years. Although many Sami people now live in modern cities, reindeer hunting is an important part of their traditional culture. Sami people raise reindeer for their meat, hides, antlers, milk, and as a form of transportation. Reindeer herders migrate with the reindeer herds from coastal regions to inland areas each year. People who do this work are called *boazovázzi*. This means reindeer walker.

forests. Today, approximately a third of Europe is still forested.

Boreal forests lie just south of the tundra in northern European countries. Rare birds such as the Ural owl and the three-toed woodpecker live in these forests. Other animals include flying squirrels, forest reindeer, and brown bears. Swamp forests lie near rivers. European white water lilies, turtles, wild boar, and frogs live in swamp forests. Deciduous trees grow in temperate forests. Deciduous trees shed their leaves each fall. Red deer, Alpine ibex, and brown bears live in these forests.

Creatures and Landscapes at Risk

Loss of habitat and pollution have damaged many of Europe's natural locations. Europeans are working to preserve some of these places and their endangered animals. For example, the Alpine ibex, a wild goat, was close to extinction. But with help from conservationists, or people who work to protect nature, the animal's numbers have increased. Other highly endangered European animals include brown bears, wolverines, and Iberian lynx.

The Iberian lynx is critically endangered due to loss of habitat.

Mediterranean forests are home to cork oak trees, Hermann's tortoises, European rabbits, and Iberian lynxes.

Grasslands

Europe's many grasslands are home to a variety of insects, reptiles, and birds. The beautiful Large Blue butterfly lives in the dry grasslands of Denmark. Other

FURTHER EVIDENCE

Chapter Three covers the plants and animals of Europe. What is one of the chapter's main points? What evidence in the chapter supports this main point? Check out the link below. Does the information on the site support the main point in this chapter? Does it raise a new point? Write a few sentences explaining how the information you found relates to this chapter.

Iberian Lynx

www.mycorelibrary.com/europe

animals that live in Europe's grasslands include birds such as the red-footed falcon, the red-backed shrike, and bustards. Land development has damaged many of Europe's grasslands, prompting the European Union to protect those areas that still remain.

Mountains

Europe's mountain regions are home to brown bears, wolves, ibex, marmots, and lynxes. Several of Europe's mountain ranges are home to the chamois, a goatlike antelope that is comfortable living in rocky, rugged areas.

CHAPTER FOUR

A LONG HISTORY

Scientists have discovered ancient cave paintings in France. These were likely painted more than 37,000 years ago. Similar paintings that might be even older have been found in Spain.

Starting around 500 BCE, the ancient Greeks and Romans built highly developed civilizations. Around 500 CE, the Middle Ages began. People call this time the middle because it connects the ancient

Ancient Scandinavians produced many runestones such as this, often to honor fallen heroes. Most runestones were created between 950 and 1100 CE.

world with the modern. This was a time when kings or other members of the aristocracy ruled most countries. Religion was an important part of everyday life for most people. Most Europeans had very little education during this time and life was very difficult.

Sometimes people call this time period the Dark Ages.

During the early 1300s, the Renaissance began. Renaissance means rebirth. The arts, science, and other discoveries blossomed in Europe during this time. The Renaissance lasted more than 300 years.

The Industrial Revolution started during the 1700s. People built

Ancient Human Ancestors in Europe

Archaeologists have found a rich fossil record of the earliest human beings in Europe. Many of these fossils were found in the caves of the Sierra de Atapuerca in Spain. Some fossils found there are as much as 886,000 years old. The remains found at this site have given scientists a wealth of information about the appearance and culture of these ancient human ancestors.

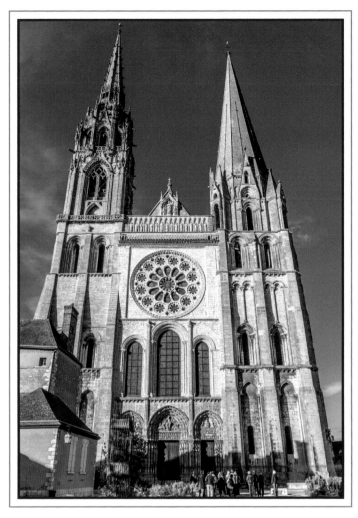

The Cathedral of Chartres, one of the greatest structures built during the Middle Ages, was constructed before the invention of modern machinery.

factories. They began using machines to produce things quickly. Europe began to focus on industry rather than farming.

Much of Europe's history, from the ages before written records to the 1900s, has been dominated by nearly constant warfare. During the 1900s, Europe

The Holocaust

The Holocaust was the mass murder of approximately 6 million European Jews during World War II. This program of state-sponsored murder was carried out by Nazi Germany and led by Adolf Hitler and the Nazi Party. The Nazis also killed members of the Romani ethnic group, disabled people, homosexuals, and Soviet prisoners of war, among others.

was devastated by World War I (1914–1918) and World War II (1939–1945). After World War II, many European countries came together to form what would later become the European Union (EU).

European Culture Today

Today Europeans celebrate many different holidays and follow a variety of customs. Easter and Christmas are important holidays for many Europeans. Many countries also have large celebrations for holy days. Soccer, called football in Europe, is extremely popular. Europeans also enjoy cricket, rugby, tennis, skiing, and boxing.

Giorgio Vasari was an Italian artist and writer who lived during the height of the Renaissance in Italy. In this excerpt from his book *Lives of the Most Eminent Painters, Sculptors, and Architects*, Vasari writes about Leonardo da Vinci's painting the *Mona Lisa*:

> *The eyes have the lustre and moisture always seen in living people, while around them are the lashes and all the reddish tones which cannot be produced without the greatest care. The eyebrows could not be more natural, for they represent the way the hair grows in the skin—thicker in some places and thinner in others, following the pores of the skin. The nose seems lifelike with its beautiful pink and tender nostrils. The mouth, with its opening joining the red of the lips to the flesh of the face, seemed to be real flesh rather than paint. Anyone who looked very attentively at the hollow of her throat would see her pulse beating. . . .*

> Source: Giorgio Vasari. The Lives of the Artists. Oxford, UK: Oxford University Press, 1998. Print. 294.

What's the Big Idea?

Take a close look at Giorgio Vasari's words. What is his main idea? What evidence does he use to support his point? Come up with a few sentences showing how Vasari uses two or three pieces of evidence to support his main point.

A UNIFIED EUROPE

Europe has the world's second-densest population, after Asia. Europe is very diverse. People have moved here from many different parts of the world. Africans have immigrated to France. Indonesians have made their homes in the Netherlands. Today people still immigrate to Europe from places such as India, China, and Ecuador.

Immigrants from all over the world have come to Europe to build new lives. These African immigrants are shopping in a street market in Marseilles on France's Mediterranean coast.

The European Union recognizes 23 official languages. German and English are widely used. Other common European languages include French, Czech, Slovak, Danish, Finnish, and Greek.

European Royalty

Twelve monarchies still exist in Europe today. A monarchy is a government with a monarch, usually a king or queen, as its head. However, most of today's European monarchies no longer play a role in governing their countries. This is an enormous change from the early 1900s. At that time monarchies ruled almost all European countries. The most famous European monarch today is Queen Elizabeth II of Great Britain. She has served as that country's queen since 1952.

The European Union

Today 27 European countries are part of the political union called the European Union. These countries work together to make rules on which they all agree. EU countries share many policies regarding free trade and economic development. Seventeen out of the twenty-seven EU countries share one currency, called the Euro.

The Louise Weiss building in Strasbourg, France, houses the European Parliament, the elected legislative body of the European Union.

People who live in the EU do not need a passport to travel to other EU countries. They are citizens of a unified Europe.

The EU allows European countries to combine their military and economic power. These countries work together on issues such as the environment and helping countries in need. EU nations work together to promote peace and democracy. This is especially important given Europe's long history of war and conflict.

Some countries in Europe are not in the EU. Some have applied or are on their way to joining. These include Iceland, Serbia, and Turkey. Others, such as Norway and Switzerland, have chosen not to

Fighting Global Climate Change

As with governments all over the world, the EU is making changes to combat global climate change. One way they are working toward this goal is by reducing the amount of energy used by buildings and appliances. EU officials believe that investing in technologies that use less energy will not only protect the environment, but also create new jobs and make Europe more competitive in world markets.

join at this time. These countries each have their own governments and currencies.

European Industry on the World Stage

Europe led the world during the development of the Industrial Revolution. It continues to be a leader in world industry today. With top companies such as Volkswagen, Mercedes-Benz, and BMW, Europe manufactures approximately a third of the world's automobiles. Europe also dominates the world's food industry. It is the largest importer and second-largest exporter of food in the world. Tourism is also an important source of income for the people of Europe.

An auto assembly plant in Mladá Boleslav in the Czech Republic manufactures Volkswagens, one of the leading brands of automobiles in the world.

Europe Today and Tomorrow

Most European cities are a combination of old and new. Cobblestone streets and ancient ruins often stand next to modern buildings. With its varied cultures and fascinating history, Europe is a wonderful place to live, work, and play!

EXPLORE ONLINE

Chapter Five focuses on the European Union. The Web site below is also about the EU. How is the information given in this Web site different from the information in this chapter? What information is the same? How do the two sources present information differently? What can you learn from this Web site?

The European Union
www.mycorelibrary.com/europe

Galleria dell'Accademia, Florence, Italy

The Galleria dell'Accademia is home to one of the world's most famous statues, *David*. Michelangelo carved this amazing marble sculpture between 1501 and 1504.

Michelangelo's statue David

Icehotel, Jukkasjärvi, Sweden

Visit this small Swedish town during the winter months to stay in a hotel made completely out of ice. This hotel is rebuilt every year because it melts in the spring!

An ice sculpture at the Icehotel

The Amalfi Coast, Italy

With its crystal-blue waters and beautiful mountains, this section of the Mediterranean coast is breathtaking.

The village of Positano on Italy's colorful Amalfi coast

Part of the elaborate gardens at Park Güell

Deep underground in the Wieliczka Salt Mine

The Parthenon temple, part of the Acropolis

Park Güell, Barcelona, Spain

Artist Antoni Gaudí designed this fantastic park, which eventually became his home. It is now open to the public.

Wieliczka Salt Mine, Kraków, Poland

This tourist destination is home to caves, underground lakes, chapels, and statues made of salt. It also boasts the world's largest mining museum and several concert halls.

The Acropolis of Athens, Greece

This area is home to several huge stone buildings built by the ancient Greeks, including the Parthenon. The Greeks built this temple in honor of Athena, the city's guardian goddess.

STOP AND THINK

Tell the Tale

Chapter Four of this book discusses the Renaissance. Imagine you are living in Florence, Italy, during the height of the Italian Renaissance. Write 200 words that tell the story of what a day in the life of a boy or girl at that time might have been like. Describe the sights and sounds around you and the people you encounter. Set the scene, develop a story, and be sure to conclude your tale.

Another View

This book has a lot of information about Europe's changing landscapes and the animals that live there. As you know, every source is different. Ask a librarian or another adult to help you find another source about the animals that live in Europe. Write a short essay comparing and contrasting the new source's point of view with that of this book's author.

Surprise Me

Chapter Three covers the plants and animals of Europe. After reading this chapter, what two or three facts about plant and animal life in Europe did you find most surprising? Write a few sentences about each fact. Why did you find them surprising?

Dig Deeper

After reading this book, what questions do you still have about Europe? Write down one or two questions that can guide you in your research. With an adult's help, find a few reliable sources that can help answer your questions. Write a few sentences about how you did your research and what you learned from it.

GLOSSARY

altitude
the height of an object or place in relation to sea level

aristocracy
the highest class in certain societies, especially those holding hereditary titles or offices

conservationist
a person who advocates or acts for the protection and preservation of the environment and wildlife

currency
coins and paper money

deciduous
trees or shrubs that lose their leaves annually

diverse
showing a great deal of variety

immigrate
to come to live permanently in a foreign country

peninsula
a piece of land almost surrounded by water or projecting out into a body of water

strait
a narrow passage of water connecting two seas or two large areas of water

tundra
a type of vast, treeless plain in the arctic regions

union
joining together or being joined together

LEARN MORE

Books

Allgor, Marie. *Endangered Animals of Europe*. New York: Powerkids Press, 2011.

Elliott, Lynne. *The Renaissance in Europe*. New York: Crabtree, 2009.

Napoli, Donna Jo. *Treasury of Greek Mythology.* Washington, DC: National Geographic Children's Books, 2011.

Web Links

To learn more about Europe, visit ABDO Publishing Company online at **www.abdopublishing.com**. Web sites about Europe are featured on our Book Links page. These links are routinely monitored and updated to provide the most current information available.

Visit **www.mycorelibrary.com** for free additional tools for teachers and students.

INDEX

ABOUT THE AUTHOR

Suzanne Francis is a children's book author and screenwriter. She lives in the Mediterranean-like city of Los Angeles, California, with her husband, Wes; their children, Jack and Emilia; and a polka-dotted dog named Lucy.